For Mark —

Celebrate The Butterflies

Presenting With Confidence In Public

Celebrate The Butterflies

Presenting With Confidence In Public

Your Nervous Energy Can Help You Speak In Public!

Stephen M. Gower

Lectern Publishing
P. O. Box 1065, Toccoa, GA 30577

First edition, published 1993 by LECTERN PUBLISHING, P. O. Box 1065, Toccoa, GA 30577.

Library of Congress Catalog Card Number: 93-79975

ISBN: 1-880150-73-5

Dedicated To Mom

There would always be extra cars in our driveway when I would come home from school!

Kool-Aid would be waiting for me on the counter. Come late spring, it would be blessed with a couple of ice cubes. A cookie or a piece of candy would lie beside the drink. Mom would be in the next room.

She would not be alone. Before I came home, another young person would have arrived. And that young man or young lady would be practicing inside with Mom. Others would be waiting their turn in the driveway.

I would sit at the kitchen table enjoying my after-school snack. And through the wall that separated den from kitchen, I would hear Mama work. Over weeks, and months, and years, I would notice improvement by young men and young women.

Mama did not teach piano. She did not tutor math. My Mama taught speech. And, I'm glad she did!

Some of my friends grew up hearing their mothers teach music. They either endured or enjoyed Chopsticks and Chopin. I grew up with "Fuzzy Wuzzy was a bear" and "she sells seashells down by the seashore."

Mother never thought it wise to try actively to teach speech to her son. But, I am undoubtedly the beneficiary of all that soaked through those walls while I ate my after-school snacks.

Mama, you gave me inflection and noun-verb agreement. You gave me intensity and spontaneity. You gave me an awesome appreciation for language. I am very proud to be your son. I will think of you everywhere and every time I speak. You will always be in the audience. And you will always be in this speaker's heart.

Thanks Mom.

Acknowledgments

Speakers are befriended by events and emotions. The one who speaks is the beneficiary of all that goes on around him, of all that transpires within him. Relationships make speakers.

I acknowledge my grandmother, who related to me in such a fashion that I was encouraged to wrestle with facts and the peril of "a little learning."

I acknowledge my students who, by the hundreds, have privileged me by allowing me to observe what can happen when confidence catches a spirit.

I acknowledge every speaker who has allowed me to contribute to the membership of the audience. When you speak as well as you do, when courage and grace are offered in equal portions, I am encouraged to dig deeper, to study more, to listen better. You are a part of every song I sing in speech.

I acknowledge my children. One times three equals a bountiful blessing of illustrations of joy.

I acknowledge my wife - the queen of encouragement, the one with whom I love to be - alone!

I acknowledge my Heavenly Father and Christ, His Son. When I speak, may they see You!

The mission of *Celebrate The Butterflies* is to provide a guide for speaking in public that is based on redirecting nervous energy in such a way that nervous energy becomes an ally to the speaker, not an enemy.

Contents

Delivering The Speech-Cake

Fly Butterfly Fly

An Introduction

STOP.
CLOSE THE DOORS.
DO NOT ENTER.
YOU ARE DELAYING THE TRAIN!

The terse words erupted from the tramway speaker system at the airport. Someone had obviously challenged the suggested methodology for boarding the train. The potential violator was being abruptly rebuffed by the mechanical verbiage.

In similar fashion, thousands of neophytes choose to wrestle against a proven approach for speaking in public. They proceed to move counter to the suggested directions and all havoc breaks loose.

Celebrate The Butterflies is an invitation to STOP the mode of thinking that categorizes nervous energy in nothing but negative terms. *Celebrate The Butterflies* presents an option that can enable you to CLOSE THE DOORS on a self-debasing technique.

Celebrate The Butterflies suggests that you MAY NOT WANT TO ENTER THE TRAIN as you have in the past. Indeed, *Celebrate The Butterflies* will present a possible change in attitude that will enable you to cease DELAYING THE TRAIN that has as its destination your significant improvement as a public speaker.

This book is not about everything in the world that has to do with public speaking. This book is about nervous energy - your nervous energy about speaking in public. By intent, *Celebrate The Butterflies* has a very narrow focus. These pages will lead you into a thorough examination of your relationship with your own nervous energy about speaking in public.

As you analyze your relationship to your nervous energy, you may recognize that you consider nervous energy as an enemy. This adversarial relationship between you and nervous energy may have resulted in many fights. Unfortunately, these battles have not occurred on neutral ground, in a far removed locale. These wars have raged deep within you. The fights resulted in wounds. The wounds still hurt. And, you remain bitter toward nervous energy.

Celebrate The Butterflies invites you to stop fighting nervous energy! Close the doors on this line of one-sided thinking. Do not enter this book with the conviction that nervous energy is always bad. Quit delaying the train that can eventually enable you to speak more confidently in public.

The crucial point of *Celebrate The Butterflies* is that the very thing that seems to bother us the most, our nervous energy, can actually bless us as we seek to speak in public.

Well, it is time to start. You are about to board a train of a different nature. This train will take you on a journey that will introduce you to STRANGER. For many of you, STRANGER is NERVOUS ENERGY. And, NERVOUS ENERGY is ENEMY.

Now, on this train ride, you will be assigned the seat right beside NERVOUS ENERGY. You will be encouraged to remain in your seat. NERVOUS ENERGY will remain seated as well.

Over the pages of this book, you will be given the opportunity to discover the other side of NERVOUS ENERGY. You then may recognize that NERVOUS ENERGY is not out to get you. NERVOUS ENERGY wants to befriend you. NERVOUS ENERGY does not want to keep you from speaking with confidence. NERVOUS ENERGY wants to help you speak confidently - in public.

Over time, over the time of this very train ride,

you may discover that NERVOUS ENERGY appears to be different. ENEMY may have become ALLY. STRANGER may have become FRIEND.

And you, yes you, may be able to identify with the note I received recently from one of my students.

> Thank you.
>
> Mr. Gower, you have helped me more than you know. As you know, I had a terrible time speaking in public. You have broken the shell that used to surround me. I do not feel so self-conscious anymore. I can be free and spontaneous in public. You have caused me to develop into the type of person I always wanted to be. I can think of no gift or reward that would measure up to what you have taught me about myself. God bless you and yours.
>
> P.S. - Watch your cholesterol. Drink lots of water.

Well, here we go! It is time that you and NERVOUS ENERGY get to know each other better. It is time for you to *Celebrate The Butterflies*!

Part One

Caterpillars No More

CHAPTER 1

The Enigma Of The Butterflies

The calendar indicates spring, and swirls of butterflies decorate the foothills of Northeast Georgia. The turf appears to be splattered with inconquerable hues of purple and black, yellow and blue, white and red.

Butterflies paint the mountains and valleys with a down-to-earth rainbow. The range of their radiant colors is challenged only by the massive variety of their size and shape.

The choreography is further enhanced by the gentle dance of the butterfly. Some seem to wiggle, others appear to waltz. All seem to dance more brilliantly in front of crowds.

Family get-togethers provide the audience that elicits encore after encore. As the size of the crowd swells, the enthusiasm level of the butterfly seems to reach a crescendo.

Whatever their routines, the butterflies appear to pour themselves equally into their presentation of dance at family gatherings.

However, members of the audience will provide responses that are not similar in nature. People will not react to the butterflies in the same way.

Toddlers will curse the butterflies with a chase. The curtain on the dance of the butterfly becomes the insides of a glass jar.

Teenagers appear to cover or ignore the activity of the butterfly with their own endeavor. The teenage ritual of romance transcends the importance of the butterfly's display of movement and color.

But one could argue that butterflies do not dance for toddlers and teenagers; butterflies frolic for you and for me. Butterflies dance for grown children.

The "oohs" and "aahs" out of the mouths of the elders feed the adrenaline of the butterfly and solicit repeat performances. Butterflies pour their wings and hearts out for us.

Their flutter triggers our flutter. The butterflies provide stimuli for our responses. And out from every nook and cranny within the Northeast Georgia mountains and valleys, there echoes the chorus "Oh how beautiful, Oh how beautiful!"

Yes, butterflies are beautiful. Butterflies are to be enjoyed. Butterflies are to be celebrated!

The Enigma

Why then would so many choose to refer to a negative sensation, an experience that is for them not enjoyable, in terms that refer to "The Butterflies"? Here is the enigma - if butterflies are good guys, then why use them, "The Butterflies," to express bad feelings or experiences?

Yet this is precisely what hundreds of thousands of people do. They refer to the feeling they get when they speak in public, or for that matter even think about speaking in public, in terms similar to the following: "I've got a bad case of the butterflies. I feel bad. I feel as if butterflies are flying all around in my stomach. Just thinking about speaking in public gives me a big, bad dose of the butterflies."

For more than a decade, my students in the college world and in business circles have used terminology similar to that listed above to indicate their nervousness, indeed in many cases nausea, about speaking in public. Over that period of time, I have often wondered why they refer to something so beautiful to describe what is obviously for them a very ugly feeling.

For some time now, I have surmised these students, and evidently thousands like them, are not referring to the beauty or appearance of the butterfly; they are relating to the fluttering of the butterfly.

Just as the butterfly may feel a vibration as he waves or flaps his wings, so my students seem to be saying that they feel some tremendous tremoring, a tossing about deep in the tummy, as they speak or think about speaking in public.

But the quick, irregular motions of the butterfly's flutter seems to produce positive results. These motions propel the butterfly from one location to another. Perhaps a hidden agenda for the butterfly's fluttering is the intriguing display of dance that it provides for an audience.

Whereas the fluttering of the butterfly yields both obvious and less apparent benefits, the quavering or fluttering deep within my students' stomachs seems to produce negative consequences. Most of the time, nothing good seems to come out of their sporadic trembling. The tremors in the tummy seem to be a curse, not a blessing.

I suspect that the very fact that you have chosen to read this book indicates that you are not unfamiliar with the negative agitation deep within one's stomach when that one is contemplating speaking in public. Perhaps you too are acquainted with "a bad case of the butterflies."

It is my hope that our time together will encourage you to take a second look at "the butterflies." "The butterflies" do not have to be dreaded. They can be celebrated. A bad case of "the butterflies" can be replaced by a good case of "the butterflies."

But first, we must analyze "the butterflies." "The butterflies," your butterflies, do not have to remain an enigma. You can begin to understand them.

CHAPTER 2

The Examination Of The Butterflies

"Who breaks a butterfly upon a wheel?"
Alexander Pope

Perhaps Pope is referring to the concept that one would not have the desire or the necessity to break or tear down a fragile butterfly upon a rough wheel. Pope was referring to real butterflies.

I am now addressing "the butterflies" in your stomach - your nervous energy about speaking in public. I am sure that you can break these butterflies down upon a wheel. And you must!

If you desire to gain confidence as a speaker, you must analyze your nervous energy. You must break down "the butterflies" and dissect your relationship to your own fluttering. Cut apart "your butterflies." Separate them into at least three segments. Examine "your butterflies."

The Family Get-Together Revisited

A return trip to the family gathering referred to in the first chapter will provide a helpful technique for segmenting "your butterflies."

You will recall that the setting for this gathering was the base of the Northeast Georgia mountains. The hills and valleys were spotted with butterflies. These frolicking splotches of color provided the stimuli for three different responses. You will remember the various responses were provided by toddlers, teenagers, and the grown children.

Toddlers would curse, chase, catch and eventually kill many of the butterflies. Their efforts to bottle-up the butterfly would sometimes backfire. Butterflies do not always play alone. An occasional wasp would dash the spirit of the toddler.

Teenagers would cover up or ignore the butterflies. The relationship between boyfriend and girlfriend would force the relationship between teenager and butterfly into one of borderline non-existence.

The grown children would be the ones to ignite the enthusiasm of the butterflies. For grown children, the butterfly was not something to be chased and caught and perhaps killed. Neither was the butterfly something to be covered up and ignored. As far as grown children are concerned, butterflies are to be celebrated.

Just as the various responses to the butterflies are represented by the toddler, the teenager and the grown child, so are the various responses to the nervous fluttering within the stomach of a would-be speaker segmented into that represented by toddlers, teenagers and grown children.

In other words, if one puts "the butterflies," the nervous energy of speakers, "upon a wheel" and breaks it down, one will notice that there are three different segments represented: the toddler, the teenager, the grown child.

Some potential speakers relate to their own nervous energy about speaking in public to the style of the toddler. Others have a relationship to their own nervous energy about public speaking in the motif of the teenager. Still others are involved with their own nervous energy in a fashion that resembles the grown child interacting with the butterflies. The grown child and the butterflies frolic together in the mountains and valleys.

For more than a decade, it has been my challenge and privilege to encourage thousands of college students and business leaders to examine their relationship to their own nervous energy as it relates to communication skills and to speaking in public.

Some have recognized a tendency to relate to their nervous energy like a toddler. They seek to chase and catch and bottle-up the nervous energy with the hope that nervous energy can be eliminated.

Others have recognized their inclination to ignore all nervous energy. Everything else, including teenage romancing, appears to be more important. If toddlers try to chase, catch and bottle-up their nervous energy, the teenagers try to cover up their nervous energy with a plethora of other activities.

I have been intrigued and encouraged by the fact that many toddlers and teenagers have become grown children through the course. Others, a very few, actually began our experience together with an appreciation, if not a celebration, of their own nervous energy.

Nevertheless, if I were to categorize all of my students, if I were to break them down into segments, I would see three: the toddler, the teenager, the grown child.

A Very Narrow Focus

Remember, these segments or categories are used to describe a speaker's relationship to his own nervous energy. This labeling, or categorization, may have nothing at all to do with other aspects of one's personhood or relationships.

For our purpose in *Celebrate The Butterflies*, "Toddler", "Teenager" and "The Grown Child" refer only to responses and relationships to one's own nervous energy about public speaking.

Let it be firmly understood that one can insist on relating to one's own nervousness about speaking in public in ways that will resemble "the toddler" or "the teenager" and be very mature, "a grown child", in every other phase or relationship in his or her life.

As a matter of fact, that is precisely what often happens. Grown children behave like grown children in every phase of their life except that aspect of their life that has to do with speaking in public. When it comes to speaking in public, children that are otherwise "grown" perceive themselves as "toddlers" or "teenagers."

Their perception may well be that they are exceptionally mature in any arena as long as the setting does not force them to speak in public.

As I write this chapter, I survey my mind's catalogue and see there many of my former students. I think now in particular of three young men and women. These particular students had two things in common with one another. Each was very attractive in appearance; each was very nervous about speaking in public.

Two of the three were destined to graduate with exceptionally high honors. A third was anticipating the extreme likelihood of a professional sports career.

All three of these very attractive young people appeared to be quite mature. However, when it came to their relationship with their own nervous energy about speaking in public, they seemed trapped in adolescence.

It is extremely important that this concept be acknowledged and claimed. One can be exceptionally mature athletically, academically, and in the area of interpersonal relationships, and still behave like a toddler or teenager in relationship to one's own nervous energy about speaking in public.

The Dissection

If your dissection of your nervous energy enables you to pinpoint the level of your relationship to this energy, then you are the recipient of a gift. You know where you are. That is a tremendous starting point!

If you perceive your relationship to your nervous energy as one that is categorized by "the toddler," if you attempt to catch and eliminate your nervous energy, then you are positioned for redirection. You recognize both your tendency to attempt to trap nervous energy and your need to rethink your relationship to this one that you perceive as ENEMY.

If you describe your relationship to your own nervous energy in terms of "the teenager" model, if you basically are ignoring nervous energy's potential power, either as enemy or friend, then you too are positioned for redirection. You may now perceive both your inclination to elude nervous energy and your need to acknowledge and embrace the presence of nervous energy.

Finally, if you understand yourself as one who behaves like a mature, grown child in relationship to his or her nervous energy, then you find yourself with an opportunity for even further development in your relationship to your friend, your nervous energy.

Your relationship to "your butterflies" may be destined toward a much deeper level of intimacy!

Whether you perceive nervous energy as enemy, stranger, or non-existent, or as a friend, you are now ready to enter a door that will enable you to take a seat and to begin a journey. On this journey, you will hopefully learn to understand your own nervous energy as new friend, or as deeper friend.

It Is Your Starting Point That Matters

Hopefully, you have now dissected and categorized your relationship to your butterflies. You have discovered your starting point.

And that is what matters for you - your starting point. We do not all have the same starting point.

You can improve your relationship to your nervous energy about speaking in public only as you pinpoint and begin to move beyond your starting point. For you, no one else's starting point is important.

Please do not beat and bash yourself by worrying about another's starting point. The starting point of another is totally irrelevant. Only your starting point is valuable to you. Your starting point is a springboard for your improvement!

CHAPTER 3

The Execution Of The Butterflies

If you want to improve your relationship with your nervous energy, if you desire to speak with confidence in public, you must understand the power of preparation.

Preparation is the key! You plan to prepare. You prepare the plan. You execute the plan, and you execute the preparation. Execution does not equal elimination. It paves the way for the proper utilization and the celebration of "the butterflies."

Transformation in the area of relationships between speakers and their nervous energy occurs when speakers learn to pay the preparation price. Pay the preparation price; anxiety may become anticipation.

A Tale of Two Nervous Energies

In recent days, I have encountered two radically different strains of nervous energy.

I choose to call one strain of nervous energy "anxiety."

Several days ago, anxiety presented itself to me in the form of a very nervous student. This particular student was about to take a very difficult test. He was nervous because he had not paid attention in class and had not studied at all for the test. He had not prepared himself. His nervous energy equaled a heavy anxiety!

The second strain is one I label "anticipation."

Anticipation revealed itself to me several days ago. Another young student was very nervous. He was nervous because he was about to marry his sweetheart of eight years.

But, in this case, nervous energy equaled anticipation. My young friend was nervous about the big move. But, he was excited because he felt that God had brought him and his soon-to-be-wife together forever. Yes, he was nervous. But, this nervous energy equaled an awesome anticipation!

Pay the preparation price, and nervous energy can equal anticipation, not anxiety. Pay the preparation price. At journey's end, dreaded butterflies will more closely resemble celebrated butterflies. Pay the preparation price. Knowledge about speaking confidently in public will benefit you!

Follow precisely the preparation plan. Execute it. Carry it out. And soon your preparation plan will help carry you into a new relationship with your nervous energy.

It is Like Baking A Cake!

Cakes are crucial to celebrations!

For centuries, cakes have been connected with celebrations. Accordingly, we will link a cake with our celebration.

The steps are simple. Another becomes hungry for a cake. You decide to bake him one. You find a recipe, mix the ingredients and bake the cake. Then you deliver the cake.

There are six steps: hunger, decision, recipe, ingredients, baking, delivery.

For our purposes, we take the six steps and group them into three categories: hunger-decision, recipe-ingredients-baking, delivery.

Six become three!

Hunger-Decision

Someone is hungry for a cake. Someone decides to bake a cake.

You can bake a speech-cake because you have something to say. Or, you can bake a speech-cake because someone asks you to say something.

Either way, somebody is hungry. Whether you bake the speech-cake for yourself or for someone else, if you are to do it, you make a decision to do it. You are no puppet on a string. You decide because you decide.

Recipe-Ingredients-Baking

Now, you choose a particular recipe - a kind of cake, a type of speech. You select the appropriate ingredients. Then, you put it all together - you bake it, you make it, you write it.

Delivery

This is terribly important!

A friend asks you to bake him a cake. You decide this is something you want to do.

You choose a recipe, secure and mix the ingredients, bake a delicious cake. But you never deliver it effectively.

You do not take the cake to him. Or, you drop it along the way. It splatters all over the place. No one ever tastes the deliciousness of your cake.

Similarly, you or someone else expresses a hunger for a speech. You decide to write it.

You choose to write a particular type. You secure and appropriately combine the ingredients. You write a powerful speech.

But, come delivery time, either you do not deliver the speech, or you deliver it ineffectively. No one ever tastes the deliciousness of your speech-cake.

It is not enough to respond to a speech hunger by deciding to write a speech. It is not sufficient merely to choose a topic and then to serve and mix the ingredients.

Merely to bake a powerful speech-cake will not satisfy the hunger. It must be delivered to the one or ones for whom it was baked.

Remember, the baking minus the delivery means no one ever tastes the speech-cake's deliciousness!

Three Become Two

For the purpose of this book, we are assuming that a hunger for a speech-cake and a decision to bake a speech-cake do exist.

Accordingly, we will focus on the recipe, the ingredients, the baking and the delivery.

More specifically, we will simply refer to the recipe, the ingredients, and the baking as "the baking of the speech-cake." Our second category will be "the delivery of the speech-cake."

And remember, throughout our journey, preparation is the key.

Caterpillars No More

Butterflies do not remain as caterpillars!

It you are in the caterpillar stage, you can move beyond that state. You can become butterfly!

Nervous energy does not have to keep you enclosed. Nervous energy does not have to limit you. Nervous energy does not have to confine you to a condition of creeping and crawling.

Just as caterpillars are vulnerable to predators, so are you open to attack as an effective speaker if your nervous energy is always working against you!

When it comes to speaking in public, you can remain a caterpillar no more!

By confronting the enigma, examining "the butterflies" and executing the plan and the preparation, you can be a creeping and crawling caterpillar no more. You can soar as an improved speaker.

Preparation, both in the baking and delivery of the speech-cake, will lead you beyond the caterpillar stage. And remember, cakes are crucial to the celebration that this very preparation makes possible.

Part Two

The Baking Of The Speech-Cake

CHAPTER 4

Show And Tell...And, Sell!

The Recipes

There are three! Basically, for our purposes, there are three speech-cake recipes or types: The Show, The Tell, and The Sell.

The Show

Here, "show" refers to the noun. The basic purpose of The Show Speech is to bring forth some sort of pleasure for the audience.

As you "put on a show," as you entertain, the audience responds.

If you accomplish your goal, the audience enjoys the experience. If you are not at all effective, the audience endures the experience.

And, for the most part, that is normally all that is expected of the audience - endure or enjoy. The speaker puts on the show!

The Tell

Here, "Tell" refers to the verb. It is what the speaker does. Normally, the speaker requests or requires no response from the audience.

The speaker has information and seeks to share that information with the audience. Basically, however, the speaker has no specific expectation of the audience.

The Sell

Personally, after having given thousands of speeches and after having heard many thousands more, I must admit the real dynamo is The Sell Speech.

Here, "Sell" refers to a very active verb, not a passive verb at all. For here, you see, the speaker is not merely presenting the show. Nor is he merely sharing data with the audience.

Sure, The Sell Speaker has information to give. And he may do it in a "showy" fashion. But he also possesses something else equally important. He has expectations of the audience.

The Sell Speaker normally wants the audience to feel a certain way and do a certain thing. He expects the audience to adopt, or adopt again, a particular feeling. He further expects the audience to take action, normally in response to a particular concept, product, challenge, opportunity or problem.

It is fundamentally important to understand that The Sell Speaker does not necessarily seek to change the mind or the actions of the audience. It is quite possible that some members of the audience already feel and act in a fashion that totally resembles the expectations of the speaker.

Nevertheless, The Sell Speaker wants the listener to feel a certain way and do a specific thing, whether the listener is already feeling and doing it or not.

Because of the dynamics of The Sell Speech-Recipe, we will focus exclusively on this type of speech throughout the book. Many will argue that it is the most challenging of these three speech types or recipes.

If one can learn to channel one's own nervous energy into working for him or her in the baking and delivery of The Sell Speech, one can certainly duplicate the basic process in the less complicated types, The Show and The Tell.

So let's get on with the show...I mean, The Sell!

CHAPTER 5

What Kind Of Cake Is That?

The Topic

Occasionally, my students become paralyzed in their search for a speech title. Just as some cakes have exceptionally inviting names, so can a creative topic intrigue the audience. So I understand and affirm some attention to the title of the speech.

But, it is much more important to select first an exciting topic. Granted, many times the topic selects you. You are asked to speak on a specific subject, or some topic grabs hold of you in such a strong fashion that you are left with no choice but to speak on that topic.

Absent concrete direction from someone asking you to speak, and absent an internal mandate from a matter of conscience, you may find the selection of topic to be one of the most difficult steps in the journey toward a thorough and effective presentation.

Whether the selection is difficult or not, it is certainly one of the most important steps. The choice of topic, the selection of subject matter, will give focus and shape to everything else you do.

Therefore, let me share five crucial observations about topic selection. These observations relate to: purpose, power, passion, patience and "particularization."

Purpose

Where do you want your audience to be when you finish your speech? What do you want them to feel? What do you want them to do?

If you do not know what you want to accomplish, you will certainly still accomplish something. You will accomplish confusion, ambiguity and perhaps even hostility on the part of the audience.

You cannot offer what you do not possess. You cannot offer certainty, clarity and conviction if you possess indecision, hesitation and fence-straddling in relationship to your topic.

If, however, you know exactly what you want your audience to feel and do, you will have a greater opportunity to accomplish your purpose. Topic selection has everything in the world to do with your purpose.

If you do not have a clear topic, do not start baking your speech-cake. Remember, you will not be able to lead your audience anywhere, if you do not even know where you are going!

Power

If you want your topic to be powerful, you must shoot with a rifle, not a shotgun!

One industry with which I am very familiar is the broadcast industry. Within that particular profession, many have celebrated the emergence of a new term - "narrowcasting." As I understand it, that term indicates a more specific focus, a more clearly defined and limited target.

Similarly, when you choose your topic, choose it in a powerful way. Choose to narrowcast.

Be specific. Be focused. Do not try to accomplish too much. Remember, power has everything to do with focusing. Power has to do with shooting a rifle. Power has to do with narrowcasting.

If you attempt to do too much, you likely will not accomplish anything.

Do not be misled into thinking that power is only influenced by quantity, volume, breadth and width. Power can best be influenced by narrow focusing!

Do not approach your topic by simply thinking that the broader the topic, the more the appeal. On the contrary, the more narrow your topic, the greater your chance of hitting your goal - a specific attitude and a concrete action on the part of the audience.

Remember, your powerful topic should look more like a rifle shot than a shotgun blast. Be narrow. Be specific. Be powerful!

For example, do not speak on "Divorce," speak on "The Effects of Divorce on the Children." Do not speak on "The Environment"; speak on "Ten Recycling Steps You Can Take to Help Protect the Environment." Do not speak on "Child Abuse"; speak on "Five Steps You Can Take to Help Alleviate Verbal Child Abuse." Do not speak on "Human Resource Development"; speak on "Perception as it Impacts Leadership." Do not speak on "Sales"; speak on "The Testimonial Letter as Your Most Powerful Sales Tool."

If you can get your audience to remember and respond to one or two fundamental points, you will be accomplishing a great deal. If you want a powerful response, then present your audience a powerful and narrow focus!

The more narrow and focused your topic, and the more condensed your content, the more effective you will be. "Narrow" is powerfully in!

Passion

Listen to your conscience!

If you are gong to speak from the heart, and I caution against speaking from anywhere else, you must listen to the beating of your own conscience. Choose a topic that interests you, invites you, inspires you. How in the world do we think we can interest another in our topic if we are obviously disinterested in it ourselves?

Passion about your topic can intensify your power and clarify your purpose!

Patience

A topic may not hit you instantaneously!

But if you seriously seek to match your topic to

the time of day, the length of meeting, the location, the occasion, the educational level of the audience and the time allotment you have been given, you will eventually be able to select a topic that meshes with the circumstances.

Given time, your patience will give you the purpose, the power and the passion that will in turn clarify your topic.

"Particularize" Your Topic

Early this year, I received quite an impressive envelope. The envelope was addressed to me and had a combination of urgent-looking stickers attached to it. I was instructed to open the envelope immediately.

Upon opening the envelope, I would learn that I was the recipient of a most unique offering. This special opportunity, I was told, was coming my way because of my good credit and my exceptional loyalty. I was informed that I was only one out of a very few who would have this opportunity.

I must admit I was moderately excited - until I looked again at the labeling on the envelope.

Sure enough, it was addressed to me at my post office box. However, beside my name were three startling words - OR CURRENT RESIDENT!

My special letter could have been received by anyone. In fact, there was nothing special about it.

"Particularize" your topic and your speech toward your audience. You want your audience to feel that you have baked your speech-cake especially for them.

If you choose to use a topic and material that you have used before, enhance your presentation with references to the make-up, needs, history and opportunity of your current audience.

Your topic should allow for "particularization." Remember, it is for them - not just any current resident. "Particularize!"

Credibility Equals Complexity Plus Acknowledgment Over Analysis

Before this chapter on topic selection is concluded, let me address the issue of complexity.

As this chapter is being written, the 1996 Summer Olympics are 1,234 days away - 1,234 days away from Atlanta!

Those of us who are proud to call ourself Georgians are finding as many different reasons to anticipate the Olympics as there are shades of peach.

My anticipation is centered around the diving

competition. I am familiar enough with the scoring for diving to understand that it is influenced by a phenomenon referred to as "the difficulty factor." The difficulty of a particular dive will influence the diver's score.

Just as Olympic judges seem to prefer difficult dives, many audiences seem to respond favorably to difficult or complex topics, if those topics are well executed.

To execute the writing and delivery of a complex topic, you will want to consider the following formula: credibility equals complexity plus acknowledgment over analysis.

I recognize that on many occasions it is extremely important to present a very simple topic. I further understand that it is beneficial to present a topic with which you are exceptionally familiar. However, I would never want to suggest that we should evade the complex nature of a difficult topic.

To the contrary, we should hit it head on. Let me go so far as to state that occasionally we should be very sure that we do not avoid sharing thoughts that are actually counter to our own thinking.

Your credibility as a speaker is enhanced, not diminished, when you acknowledge to your audience the complex nature of your topic, or the complexity of a particular issue related to your topic.

If you're dealing with a difficult, or even controversial topic, acknowledge the fact. As you acknowledge and analyze the complexity of a particular issue, you will be enhancing your believability.

If, for example, you are delivering a presentation that favors massive expenditures on outer space exploration, then the effectiveness of your speech will be enhanced if you admit that there are counterviews. You acknowledge the fact that there are arguments contrary to your position.

You then point out any inconsistency or shortsightedness in that thinking. When you do this, you have not argued the other side; you have buffeted your position by facing up to, rather than superficially avoiding, the complexity of a particular issue.

And, in the eyes and ears and hearts of most of your audience, you have enhanced your credibility as a speaker.

Lose yourself in the complexity of your topic. Immerse yourself into its difficulty, and serendipity will touch you. Your nervous energy will equal anticipation, not anxiety. A complex topic can befriend you!

CHAPTER 6

It Is More Than A Triple Decker

The Layers

Before we focus on the ingredients of the speech-cake, it is very important to understand how many layers, or parts, we will have in The Sell Speech.

Something will have to hold all of these ingredients together. We need some type of layer pan, we need some way to compartmentalize the ingredients.

Our physical bodies are held together by the skeleton. Our speech will have something to hold it together - the outline.

The Outline Has Five Layers

Though there can be many modifications to this particular outline paradigm, I think it is a tremendous starting point.

The five-layered outline that we will focus on includes: the introduction, the problem/opportunity, the double analysis, the remedy/response, and the conclusion.

The body of the speech will have as its center a particular opportunity or problem. We will paint a mind picture of this opportunity or problem. We will define it, tell what it looks like. Then we will analyze why the problem or opportunity exists. We will then ask specifically what has caused it to happen or occur. Finally, in the body, we will suggest for the audience a particularized response or remedy.

The Introduction

But we just do not jump into our problem or opportunity. We do not simply start a speech. We introduce a speech.

One of the most common mistakes my students make is in this area. They do not introduce their speeches. They start them.

Most of the time, we would never think of asking someone to go somewhere with us without telling them where we are going. We would normally not invite someone on a trip without telling them the destination.

But many times that is precisely what happens when it comes to speaking. We blatantly expect our audience to listen actively to our presentation without telling our audience where we are headed.

Do not just start your speech. Introduce it!

The Glue, The Grabber, The Invitation

The effective introduction has three ingredients: a glue, a grabber, and an invitation. You must have all three. A super glue and a terrific grabber will in no way excuse the absence of an invitation.

The Glue

The introduction must offer clarity. It must state what the journey will be, describe where the destination is and, to a degree, give some clue about the expectations the speaker has of the audience.

I am well aware that some introductions that do nothing more than arouse the curiosity of the audience are very effective. But they are the exception, not the rule.

The introduction should have something to do with the speech. It should "stick to," relate to the body of the speech. Do not introduce Jane if you're going to talk about Tarzan.

Just remember this. The introduction must have some glue so it can stick to the body and to the conclusion. The introduction must contribute to the overall purpose and tone of the speech. It must stick to and adhere to the rest of the speech.

The Grabber

Not only should the introduction possess glue, it must accomplish a second purpose. It must grab the attention of the audience. The introduction must hook the audience.

When you are speaking, you are fighting for the listener's mind. You are up against some rather stiff competition.

Some of your audience will be preoccupied with sick relatives. That is where their mind will be - on their relatives. Others will be tired. Their mind will be on their fatigue.

Some may have just failed tests, recently lost big clients, or just received speeding tickets. Failure and disappointment will be eager to invade their minds and dominate their thought-life during your speech.

Others will be "in love," or at least "in like." Preoccupation with their special relationship may be so powerful as to diminish any inclination to listen to your speech.

Because of the massive competition for your listeners' minds, it is very important for you to work hard to grab their attention. Remember, you will be in a battle for their mind. This war will be waged on a field called "introduction."

You must get their attention early. Hook them. Use a creative introduction that grabs.

But remember, it must certainly relate to the topic!

The Invitation

The last level of the introduction is the invitation. Your introduction should relate to your topic. It should grab, or hook, the attention of the audience. Finally, it should seek to keep the attention of the audience.

The introduction gets the attention of the audience and seeks to keep that attention. It hooks their attention for a purpose - additional attention. It gets them on the hook. It seeks to keep them on the hook.

In the past, I have found very effective introductions to include, but not be limited to, the following: personal stories, striking statistics, current events, powerful quotations, poems, and a series of direct statements.

Whatever the form, the introduction is effective if it has glue - that is, if it sticks to the rest of the speech, if it grabs the attention of the audience and if it invites further attention.

This third element, a direct or indirect invitation for the listener to commit to listening, is very important.

The Body

The body of The Sell Speech will have three levels, each building on the prior level, and each related to a central problem or opportunity.

The first level of the body paints a picture of a particular problem or opportunity that has just been introduced. This first tier tells what the problem or opportunity looks like, what it has done, what it is doing, what it may do, whom it is hurting, or whom it may help.

The first level resembles the patient describing what hurts to the doctor. The patient tries to paint a picture of the problem for the doctor.

Similarly, here the speaker paints a picture of the vanishing ozone layer, the driver who drinks, the sagging sales figures, the depressed teenager, the starving third world.

The second level of the body of The Sell Speech is a double analysis of the problem or the opportunity. Just as a doctor analyzes the picture the patient has painted so the doctor can write instructions for improvement or modification, the speaker analyzes the problem or opportunity at two points.

Basically, in the second level of the body, the double analysis, the speaker answers these two questions. Why is this happening? Why is it bad (or good)?

- Why is it bad that the ozone layer is getting a big hole in it, and why is it happening?
- Why is it bad that drivers drink and drive at the same time, and why do they do it?
- Why is it bad that sales are down for last year, and what is causing the sales slump?
- Why is it bad that many teenagers are so discouraged these days, and why are they so discouraged?

- Why does it matter that the third world is hungry, and why are they starving?

The third level of The Sell Speech is a response/remedy. The first two levels, if effectively written and presented, should encourage a certain percentage of your audience to feel a certain way. This third level is designed to build upon that feeling and is further constructed so as to lead the audience to do a certain thing.

Just as the doctor seeks to lead the patient to take action, whether it is to be swallowing prescription pills, undergoing surgery, or exercising, the speaker points the audience toward a remedy, a solution, a curative. The speaker seeks to elicit an active response.

Examples of the above may look and sound like this:

- Specifically, this is what you can do to help protect the ozone layer!
- These are precise steps you can take to discourage drinking and driving!
- Our sales will increase if you will do these things!
- You can help teenagers in these ways!
- You can help the starving third world by following this ten-step course of action!

Red Flag

Do not underestimate the power of this third level - the response/remedy. Do not paint a picture of something troubling or challenging and then stop there. Do not analyze why its occurrence is bad and analyze why it is happening and then stop there.

Do not just get us excited or perplexed. Give us something to wish for and something to do!

Your tendency will be to paint and analyze the picture and forget the third level. Please do not do that.

Follow through! Follow all the way through. Do not leave us hanging.

Spell out in "particularized" fashion what we can do. Be very specific. Specificity at this third level of the body makes The Sell Speech.

The Conclusion

If you have real good stuff in your speech, and if you want to know where the best place to put that real good stuff is, then I suggest you consider the conclusion.

You could possibly place your best material in the introduction, body - level one, body - level two, or body - level three. But I certainly hope you will give just consideration to the conclusion.

The conclusion may not always be the best place for your best data, but most of the time it will be.

I suspect that if you choose to place your best data somewhere other than the conclusion, you will select the introduction. Certainly, the very first impression you make on your audience and the last impression you leave with them are both supremely important. But remember, this last impression, your conclusion, is that special time when you revisit for your audience the essence of your speech!

As I write this particular chapter of *Celebrate The Butterflies*, I am headed for Bismarck, North Dakota. Currently, our plane is approaching Salt Lake City.

If you've never viewed Salt Lake from many miles high, you've missed one of God's special creations.

To me, Salt Lake is unique because of the way it mirrors all that is above - sky and plane and bird. I understand that perhaps only one other lake, that one being in Jerusalem, rivals Salt Lake in its capacity to reveal a reflection of all that is above, of all that goes before.

Just as Salt Lake reflects, your conclusion should reveal a reflection. It should reflect all that has gone before. It revisits the sky of your speech. It catches again the central thrust of your presentation.

Certainly your conclusion, in the midst of its reflection of the central thrust of your topic, should present an attitude of hope. You want your conclusion to be positive.

Certainly your conclusion seeks to help the audience bottle-up the essence of what you said, how they feel, and what they now must do. But remember, it is very helpful toward the accomplishment of that specific task if you end on a hopeful rather than a dismal note.

Aided by your conclusion, you hope that your audience is hopeful!

Let me add that I have occasionally found it very helpful for the conclusion to refer back to the introduction. If my introduction presented a certain set of circumstances in a state of despair, then my conclusion may paint a picture of the same situation within a state of hope.

An Example

Let me now share a thumbnail example of how

you might approach this technique.

You are a manager responsible for two hundred supervisors. Together, these supervisors are responsible for more than one thousand and five hundred workers. More specifically, each supervisor is responsible for seven to eight people.

You have been studying employment figures and have observed something startling. Within the last two years, one hundred and sixty-two people have quit working with your company. That is far too many!

You decide something must be done to reduce the turnover. You call for a meeting of your two hundred supervisors.

You decide that you will directly speak to them. You begin to write your speech - your sell speech, your five-part speech.

I. You will introduce your presentation.

II. You will present the situation and paint a picture for your audience.

III. You will analyze the situation. You will seek to express the reasons why the situation has developed and the reasons why the situation is so bad.

IV. You share a reaction that you expect. You call for a response. You seek a remedy.

(Note - if this situation were good, you of course would ask for a response, a positive reaction, not a remedy.)

V. You conclude.

In a very thumbnail fashion, let me illustrate how you might compartmentalize your speech. Let me remind you again that this is a very sketchy approach.

I. Introduction - In 1990, the Atlanta Braves were last in their division. For the next two years, they would be playing in the World Series. The Atlanta Braves reversed a trend. So must we!

II. The situation. - Within the last two years, we have lost more than ten percent of our workforce. Forty-five people have turned in resignations just in the last three months. Of those who have quit, more than one-half have been with us more than five years. We must reverse the trend.

III. The Double Analogy (The reasons) - Why is this turnover happening? Why is it a trend that must be reversed? According to our post-employment surveys, these people are quitting because of two reasons. They think we do not care about the quality of our product anymore. They think we certainly do not care about them. This trend must be reversed, because if it continues we will not be in business.

IV. The response - this is what we must do. What I need from you is a certain attitude - an attitude of concern. I also need you to do the following three things:
   1. Attend our new consistent quality improvement course that will begin next week and run for three months.
   2. Purchase and read one of the books from this special managerial book list that I will give you later.
   3. Encourage your supervisees at the point of their strengths. Also, please keep a log of your specific encouragement efforts toward each of your supervisees.

V. Conclusion - The Braves were not the only team playing in the 1991 World Series who had been last in their division the year before. The Minnesota Twins had also been in last place in their division in 1990. In 1991, the Twins won the World Series. Ladies and Gentlemen, we need a grand slam! We need to win the Big One. Our company and your supervisees are counting on you. Batter Up!

The Gift Of Structure

Organize and write your speech with the gift of structure in mind!

You cannot deliver what you do not have. You can deliver what you do have.

Gift yourself with the benefit of structure, and you will encounter welcome road signs along the delivery-way of your speech.

Make it easy on yourself to recognize the segments, the progressive steps within your speech.

It will naturally follow that your audience will have a greater opportunity to follow your speech if you can follow it yourself.

If you are ambiguous about your speech purpose, what in the world causes you to think that your audience will ever discover clarity in the midst of your ambiguity? If you make it easy on yourself to recognize sequential road signs along the way of a speech, your audience will be likely invited to follow the path you lay.

Mystery Meat

Let us know where we are headed!

Most of the time, most of us like to know where we are headed.

That was almost impossible during my college experience. As a matter of fact, many days my college classmates and I would forego our attempts to classify a particular portion of meat as beef, pork, poultry or fish. In desperation, we would often resort to labeling the portion of a stringy substance served at the school cafeteria as "mystery meat." We would be forced to wonder where the eating of the meat would take us.

When an audience gets ready to listen to a speech, they want to know where the speech will take them. I recognize the value of the surprise effect in a presentation. I understand that curiosity can indeed invite attention. But for the most part, you will be wise to make as clear to your audience as possible the destination. They have a right to know where they are headed.

There should be little mystery about it!

Not only will you and your audience benefit from clarity about your purpose and topic, both you and your audience will benefit when the sequential movement from introduction to body to conclusion is separate and clear.

When you deliver your presentation, make it easy to follow the sequence of the speech. Let us see the steps. Allow us to follow the sequential and progressive movement. Help us move from introduction to conclusion.

Hold our hand along the way. Nurture us. Let us know what's coming next. Engage us.

Clarity of purpose and sequence will help you! It will also benefit the audience. Do not serve them "mystery meat." Bless your speech with the gift of structure!

CHAPTER 7

Meat On Bones

The Icing

We have just covered the basic five-point outline of the sell speech: introduction, body - level one, body - level two, body - level three, conclusion. You will recall that earlier in the book we compared the outline of the speech to the skeleton that holds your body together, to the bones that form and shape your body.

You need a fundamental outline, the five layers, to bake a speech-cake. But, you need more than just the bones of the speech.

Just as there is meat on the bones of your body, so must there be meat, or icing, on the bones of your speech-cake.

The basic structure and fundamental points of your speech equal bones. The other content of your speech equals meat on bones.

By pure definition, I refer to "meat on bones" as elaboration, extension, explanation, substance, stuff - the hinges that open the door toward the audience's basic understanding of your speech.

As you gain confidence in using "meat on bones" in your speech, you will be taking significant strides in rethinking your attitude toward your own nervous energy. As you channel your nervous energy toward discovering and utilizing creative "meat on bones" techniques, you will be moving from aimless worrying to a more creative use of "your butterflies." You will be channeling or directing "your butterflies" toward creativity!

There are numerous ways to elaborate. You can take a basic point and explain that point in a plethora of ways. The hinges that open doors of understanding take different shapes.

The various types of "meat on bones" can help you add substance to your basic outline in such a way that your audience wants to keep listening, rather than to ignore. The different types of "meat on bones" not only help you keep the attention your audience, they can lead to the audience's understanding of the fundamental concepts of your speech.

"Meat on bones" can help you keep the attention of the audience, and "meat on bones" can help you achieve understanding by the audience.

And, "meat on bones" helps you. It serves as a road map, as a guide, that actually helps you get through your speech. "Meat on bones" serves as road signs for the speaker. Whether the speaker uses notes, or presents the speech note-free, the various types of "meat on bones" help trigger each other, dictate progression, enable the speaker to know what comes up next.

What Does Meat On Bones Look Like?

We've examined the bones of the speech-cake, our five-layered outline. Now, let's get specific and learn what "meat on bones" can look like.

The Illustration

It can look like an illustration. So, let me illustrate.

As I write this particular portion of this chapter, I'm on a Delta jet headed for another presentation. It is 10:45 p.m. Eastern Standard Time and a good while ago the lighting panel above me ceased to function. There were no lights, and I could not continue my writing.

Several minutes passed. I asked the attendant about the situation. He told me they were trying to figure out the problem and hoped to remedy it soon.

More time passed. I continued to sit in a state of mild frustration.

The attendant entered the cockpit and had a lengthy conversation with the pilot about the dilemma. After more time, the attendant came to me and again said they had not yet fixed the lights.

Then he said "the biggie."

"You know, the lights are only out on your side," he said.

There were to my right, on the other side, six empty seats. Each had light panels that functioned. They never became inoperative.

For close to twenty minutes, there was available light less than three yards away from where I sat in darkness. I could have turned on one of several light panels and sat right underneath it the whole time. But, I continued to sit in the dark.

Just as I sat in the frustration of darkness when available light was so close by, many speakers sit in frustration because they do not know how to explain their point. But help, "meat on bones," is so close by. "Meat on bones" is light that is so close by. "Meat on bones" is all around you. It is life. It is circumstances and statistics. It is current events and stories. It is so close by - just as the lighting panels on the other side of my plane were close by.

But, just as I assumed all lights were out, we as speakers many times assume we are out of ways to explain our point. Just as I did not know the other side's lights would work, many of us do not know that our circumstances, our study, our weirdness and all our "inside and outside stuff" will work to help us keep the attention of the audience. And, it will work to help us make our point.

The "Just As" Stuff

You may have noticed by now that my favorite type of "meat on bones" is what I refer to as the "just as" stuff - just as I did not know the other side's lights were available to me, many speakers do not know that their everyday experiences will work as "meat on bones."

But everyday experiences, like my plane trip tonight, are not the only type of "just as" stuff that you can use to elaborate, to explain, to extend your point.

There are many types of "just as" stuff that can serve as hinges to help you open the door of understanding for your audience. There are several ways for you to turn to a word, a person, an event, a poem, a song, a set of numbers, a story, a movie, a cartoon, a quote and then find a way to explain your point. And it is all "just as" stuff!

A Word

Frog	I observed a frog the other day. That frog could not keep still. Why, he'd jump from one lily pad to another lily pad to another lily pad. Just as that frog would jump from lily pad to lily pad, so do we. We do not know how to focus on one lily pad at a time.
Mosquito	Ever notice how small a mosquito is? But what an aggravation a mosquito can cause. And, if you are not careful, little bitty worries can become big aggravations, just as the little bitty mosquito can bring on big pain.

Pencil Eraser	Just as the eraser can eliminate our mistakes, so does Jesus Christ erase our mistakes if we earnestly believe and seek His forgiveness.
Beaver	Just as the beaver gradually and carefully builds his dam, so can you gradually and carefully build a powerful presentation that will stand firm against the rushing waters of criticism.
Salt	Just as salt adds a special zest to corn on the cob, so does "meat on bones" add a special flavor to your speech. Salt helps your food taste better. "Meat on bones" can help your audience listen better and understand better.
Air	Just as air is there even though you cannot see it, so is God's spirit with you even though you cannot see Him.

Beard	Just as some people grow a beard to cover up a scar on their chin, many of us act real egotistical just to cover up a real scar with our own poor self esteem.

The function, appearance, or sensation represented by the word helps you build an analogy to illustrate a point. As you should have noticed from the illustrations above, almost any word can give you great "just as" stuff.

A Person

Abraham Lincoln	Just as Abraham Lincoln was defeated time and time again before he was elected President, so can you overcome defeat and move toward victory.
Stevie Wonder	Just as Stevie Wonder was encouraged at the point of his strength, his gift of ear, so can someone else be encouraged by you at the point of their strength.

Helen Hayes	Just as Helen Hayes overcame her handicap, so can you.
Winston Churchill	Just as Winston Churchill indicated his own concern for persistence in his "Never Give Up" speech, and just as Winston Churchill illustrated that persistence in his life, so can you.

It may be helpful to note that the person you use to illustrate your point does not have to be famous. Of course, the use of a well-known personality is beneficial because the audience may likely be familiar with him or her and hence be more inclined to make the connection, or catch the surprising fact, you are trying to illustrate.

However, some of your most powerful "just as" stuff may come by the way of someone very close to you, but unfamiliar to your audience. Though the specific person may not be known by your audience, each of us is aware of how funny, perceptive, and downright interesting our friends and family members can be. For example, the spontaneity of a speaker's child has been responsible for thousands of illustrations by that particular speaker.

An Event

'91 World Series	Just as the 1991 World Series featured two teams that were last in their divisions the year before, the Atlanta Braves and the Minnesota Twins, so can you move from last place in the area of confidence about speaking in public. And, with preparation, you can become champion of your own nervous energy.
'96 Olympics	In the same way Atlanta shocked much of the world by becoming host city for the 1996 Olympics, so can you work day to day and ultimately and effectively carry the torch for your cause through your presentation skills.

You may notice by observing the language in the last illustration that the phraseology you use does not always have to be "just as." Words like "in the same way" and "similar" and "similarly" will work just as well.

A Wrap-Up

Just as a word, a person, and an event can serve as effective "meat on bones," so can a poem, a song, a set of numbers indicating a trend, a story, a movie, a quote serve as hinges to help open the door of understanding for your audience.

And just as the "just as" stuff is helpful, so can "unlike" stuff be beneficial. With "unlike" stuff you simply move in the other direction.

The Bodybuilder	Unlike the bodybuilder who works diligently to build his biceps, most of us slumber on the sofa and sit around waiting for happy endings.
The Turtle	Unlike the turtle who paces himself toward an accomplishment, we hurry up and make mistake after mistake.

Remember that "just as" stuff, and for that fact "unlike" stuff, will help you explain, elaborate and make your point.

Skinny Speeches Will Be Chosen Last

When I was much younger, I was one skinny character. I actually looked like a pencil with an eraser on top. Now, I more closely resemble a pencil with an eraser in the middle - the middle being the tummy.

But when I was young, I did not like being skinny. My skinny status would mandate the coaches and the neighborhood captains to choose me last when teams were being picked.

Just as my skinny status held me back from accomplishing what I wished I could have achieved, a bony, meatless speech will not move your audience. Just as my skinny status did not move the coaches, so will skinny speeches fail to encourage or inspire audiences.

Do not give your audience anything but skin and bones. Put meat on those bones. And remember, "just as" stuff will help.

But, do not take the "just as" stuff too far!

Illustration Heavy

This is another example of a strength being taken too far!

As important as "just as" stuff is, as helpful as illustrations are, it is still necessary to note that they can be taken too far.

Certainly, it is not only effective, but necessary, to put meat on bones in the form of illustrations and examples. But, be careful here.

You can seek to bless your presentation with many illustrations. But watch out, many may soon become too many. And too many examples or illustrations will curse, not bless, your presentation.

This particular warning, this part of the book, is being written at the Royal D'Iberville in Biloxi, Mississippi. I arrived several hours early; I am using this free time to work on the book.

Considering the fact that I am just moments away from speaking for the National Safety Council, and considering the fact that I am trying right now to illustrate the danger of excessive illustration, I find it most helpful to state for you what I just observed.

The folks here were kind enough to position me in a conference room so I would be able to write during the waiting period. This particular conference room features five windows, all of which focus on the Gulf.

So, I have frequently been tempted to glance away from the yellow pages of legal pad into the white of sand and the blue of ocean. My last glance revealed something quite interesting.

While I was glancing at the ocean, I observed a moving vehicle on the beach. The unusual thing was this - the door behind the driver was still open. After several seconds, the vehicle stopped, the driver reached back and shut the door behind him, then proceeded to drive away.

Now, you might say that there is nothing really unusual in that. Observed by itself, outside my particular circumstances, I would agree with you. I have even driven off with both door and trunk flapping in the wind.

But, given this particular set of circumstances, the specific point I am trying to make here and the upcoming presentation for the National Safety Council, I found the occurring of the dangling door both uncanny and timely.

The back, or the backbone, of your speech is its basic theme, its fundamental reason for existence. The very fabric or reason of the speech is the core, the center - the backbone.

Unfortunately, many times we do not close the back door. We take a strength too far.

We worry more about the icing, the front door, than we do the body of the cake. We focus so excessively on illustrations that the backbone is diluted, left open.

Illustrations should help you make your point, not camouflage it!

Do not become so preoccupied with the illustrations up front that you fail to close the door in the back. Do not become so preoccupied with your examples that you fail to make the point, move the audience, sell the product, reverse a trend. Keep your first goal in first place in your mind. The basic objective of your speech is your first priority.

Illustrations should not be the focus. Illustrations should point to the focus. Do not leave focus dangling. Present it. Make it. Do it. Close it!

CHAPTER 8

Brewing A Brainstorm

Rainbow Cake

You have decided to write a speech. You understand the fundamentals of speech organization. You understand what your topic is to be. You understand the parts of a speech. You comprehend "meat on bones." What you do not understand is what you are to do next.

You are to brew a brainstorm! Brainstorms do not just happen, they are brewed.

But how do you brew a brainstorm?

When I was much younger, and slimmer, I enjoyed Neapolitan ice cream - three flavors in one. Rainbow Cake is seven flavors in one. To brew a brainstorm, you bake a Rainbow Cake.

You become a R-A-I-N-B-O-W person! You research, assemble, investigate, narrow, build, obligate and watch!

Research

This may not be the typical definition of brainstorming. For our purposes, brainstorming is looking inside your brain, and looking outside your brain into the brains of others. More specifically, you research inside and outside for material.

You look inside. If you have a "precious folder," you use it. If you do not have such a folder, you make one. You store your precious experiences. You save notes you have received, thoughts you have had, circumstances that have touched you.

Your precious folder will serve you for a lifetime. It will function as a forever expanding catalogue of you and your experiences. You should contribute to your precious folder every time something unique happens to you or is observed by you.

You research inside. You brainstorm inside. You research your own personal and precious folder.

You research outside. You interview others. You borrow, with permission and/or documentation, their preciousness. You watch movies and visit libraries. You listen to tapes and you read books.

The topic you have chosen, or the topic that has selected you, will mandate the direction of your inside and outside research - of your brainstorming!

Assemble

You bring together all of your inside and outside stuff and you lay it on a table, or place it on the floor.

If you do not have everything that you expect to have, but feel compelled to begin the assembly process, then put in the pile a labeled index card that indicates any additional soon to come item.

This is the phase when you try to bring all of your stuff into one big pile. You assemble.

Investigate

You seek to find out if the material is what you want it to be.

Your material is laying in front of you in a big pile. Item by item, you investigate this material!

- Material - if you were married to my topic, would you and my topic get along with each other? Will you help my topic to do what I want it to do? Or, material will you hurt my topic?

- Material - if you were married to my audience, would you and my audience get along with each other? Do you confess to being over their head? Do you confess to being so simple that the audience would be offended by you? Material - are you suited for this audience on this day in this place?
- Material - if you were to be married to truth, would you and truth get along?
- Material - are you correct?
- Material - if you were married to me, could we make it together? Material - do you stand for something that I cannot stomach? Can I share you and still be filled with integrity? Material - are you my enemy? Or, are you my friend?

During this investigatory phase, you put your material to the test!

Narrow

This is the toughest phase. Here, you eliminate the material that did not pass your investigation, your test. In some cases, you throw out material that passed every question but one.

I know that throwing out, if only just for this speech, is a tough thing to do. I have thinned enough Silver Queen corn rows to be familiar with the pain of narrowing!

But I know that removing tiny, strong, healthy corn stalks makes it possible for other strong, healthy corn stalks to grow better and to produce more corn.

If great corn on the cob is the goal, then thinning is in! If a great, focused and powerful presentation is the goal, then narrowing is in.

Here, you thin out any inappropriate or superfluous data. You cull away the material that does not pass the investigation; you put your material through an ordeal. If it makes it, then fine. If it does not make it, then it should not have made it, and that is fine too.

But when you have done that, you have done only one-half of your narrowing!

The second phase of narrowing is sorting your material into the specific part of the speech in which you plan to use it. You'll have fun with this part!

I have found the simplest way to narrow or sort in this phase of brainstorming is to take the pile of research material that has been assembled and investigated and place it piece by piece into one of five smaller stacks. Again, I have found a large table or the floor very suitable for this process.

You simply place your material in one of five stacks labeled accordingly:

I - Introduction
II - Body - Level One (Problem/Opportunity)
III - Body - Level Two (Analysis/Analysis)
IV - Body - Level Three (Remedy/Response)
V - Conclusion

This process takes a lot of practice. But eventually, you pick up a knack for matching a particular piece of information, or a specific illustration, with one of your five stacks or parts. Remember, you are brewing a brainstorm. You're trying to build your speech.

The procedure works like this. One by one, you take your material pieces and ask questions similar to the following:

- Would this quote be better in the introduction to help grab their attention? Or, would it be better to place it in stack number five, in the conclusion, as a way to help the audience recapture my basic theme?
- Are these statistics best used in stack number two? Are they helpful in painting a picture of the problem or opportunity? Or, would it be better to use these statistics in stack number

four to explain a response or a very specific remedy?

- Is the best place to use this story about Abraham Lincoln here, in stack number two, to help paint a picture of the opportunity for hope in the midst of a desperate situation? Or would it be best to place it in the next stack, stack number three, to help me analyze why a situation has developed and why it is bad?

Narrowing your material, eliminating portions of your material and then sorting the remaining data into stacks, helps position you for the next rainbow step.

Build

As you sort, you're actually beginning to build each of your five parts - the introduction, the three different parts that make up the body, the conclusion.

This sorting leads to structure. The structure supports additional material.

The structure eventually becomes strong enough to allow you to move your material from one stack to the other stack.

Eventually, as you build, and as you compare how the different options sound and look, you become convinced that "this is where it belongs in the speech-building."

Obligate

And once you are convinced, you obligate - "I will build my speech with this material in this stack, in this place."

Watch

The final rainbow stage is a celebration. You celebrate the procedure because it has worked. And you have watched it work.

But there is something more important to celebrate than the fact that the procedure worked. You also celebrate the fact that your nervous energy has worked. It has worked for you. And perhaps, more than anyone else, you have been privileged to watch your nervous energy work for you. Personally, you have watched it all happen.

You not only watch the procedure working, you watch your nervous energy working. And now, you like what you see.

Pour yourself into this process. Watch what happens. Nervous energy is becoming your friend.

Practice being a rainbow person!

Before we move on here, I feel compelled to remind you that the rainbow process is a series of series. You may have to do it more than one time for the same speech.

But all the while, you are building. You're chiseling, you're sculpting - because you are a rainbow person.

As a rainbow person, you are a collage of many different hues - a composite of researching and assembling, of investigating and narrowing, of building and obligating, and of watching!

I encourage you. Look for the rainbow within you!

Thought Evaporation

Before we move to the delivery of the speech, let me urge you to write down any R-A-I-N-B-O-W or illustration ideas as soon as you discover them.

Be leery of thought evaporation. Do not allow the icing to melt!

Our driveway is constructed so that water has a tendency to accumulate in one particular spot. Come even a light sprinkle, and within a matter of minutes, a puddle will be born.

But the impressive thing is not so much the speed with which the water accumulates as it is the rapid rate at which the puddle can evaporate.

If a great concept comes to your mind, write it down - right then. If you observe a funny occurrence and think there may be a story in that happening, write it down - right then. If a song, a poem, a movie grabs you, then grab a pen and write down what you want to remember, or write down a reminder to secure a piece of the work - but do it right then.

Over a period of several hours, many different illustrations or ideas may form a puddle within your head. Do not trust that puddle to last long. It will evaporate before you know it.

So write down those concepts and illustrations and ideas. Write them down - right then!

Create A Catalogue

Write them down, even if you do not have a particular need for them at the time.

Years ago, one of my neighbors hauled into his backyard two huge barrels, or drums. He placed them underneath the overhang of a tin roof that covered his utility shop.

Heavy rains would come. People would begin to complain about the excessive amount of water we were receiving.

My neighbor would not complain. He would just collect and store that excess water, even if he did not need it right then.

Soon, our now famous drought would come, and those who just weeks ago complained about the flooding were now flooding to my neighbor's house to borrow water.

Write your newly-discovered concepts or illustrations down immediately - before the drought comes. Do not allow them to evaporate just because you do not need them now. Their time will come.

I have found that a great idea or illustration can possess two exceptionally important qualities.

The first quality is represented in the fact that some illustrations are so classical in nature that they can persevere over time. They can easily be preserved if you simply write them down.

The second great quality that some illustrations hold is that they are unusually flexible. This means that the same illustration or concept may be used in more than one speech, and in more than one place within the same speech.

Write your conceptual or illustrative ideas down immediately, even if you do not need them immediately. Build your inventory of ideas. Create a catalogue!

Part Three

Delivering The Speech-Cake

CHAPTER 9

Deliver The Cake!

Can They Taste It?

Earlier, we were comparing public speaking to cake baking. We said that it would be ridiculous to bake a delicious cake for someone and then not deliver it to them. They would never be able to enjoy the delicious cake.

In like fashion, it is extremely ridiculous and ultimately ineffective to write an excellent speech-cake and then not deliver it well. The audience will not be able to experience the deliciousness of your speech-cake. It will not profit you or your audience if you write a great speech but do not deliver it effectively.

Let your nervous energy help you write your speech; allow your nervous energy to help you deliver your speech. Pour your nervousness into your speech both at the point of writing and at the delivery place. Prepare to write; prepare to deliver.

Face It - Your Eyes Carry You!

One of the most fundamental things I can tell you about speaking in public, about the delivery of your speech, is that your eyes are very important. And it is essential that you first understand this before we focus further on the delivery of the speech.

Your eyes can work for you or they can work against you. Let your audience see your eyes and your face. Let them observe your sincerity, your credibility, your believability, your passion, your intensity, your personality.

Now, if your eyes are going to work for you, if your audience is going to see your eyes, and for that fact your face, you must be familiar with your speech. You must know it well enough so that your eyes do not constantly look at your notes, if you have notes. Your audience will not see your eyes and face if your eyes and face are pointed down toward the podium; nor will they hear your words if your mouth is aimed down.

I have worked with students and business leaders who want to learn to speak with confidence in public for a long time. I understand that one does not always refuse to look at the audience because that one has to look at the notes of the speech.

You can be very familiar with your speech and still not want to look at your audience. I know that.

I understand that many are hesitant to look at the audience for another reason other than the necessity to look at the notes or the manuscript of the speech. Some are simply afraid to look at an audience face to face.

This Will Help

If you recognize a tendency to look away from your audience, not because you need to see your material, but because you are uncomfortable with looking at your audience and seeing them looking at you, then I suggest you analyze something right now.

Face It

This analysis, perhaps as much as any other one thing that we will do, may well essentially lead you to claim your nervous energy as ally, not villain.

The analysis has as its center a series of questions: What is it that has power over you? What are you afraid of? If what you are worried about happening actually happens, then so what?

Over the years, for much more than a decade now, I have encouraged my students, both in the college and business setting, to take the journey that involves asking and answering the aforementioned questions. Usually, I discover the same answers: "I'm nervous. My nervousness is controlling me. I have a bad case of the butterflies. I'm afraid of making a mistake. I'm afraid I will look like a fool. They may not like me."

Now, that last statement, "they may not like me" is extremely interesting, and it is a key to this process of analysis.

An Interesting Surprise

It is my perception that we give too much power to "what other people think." And, I am now quite sure that much of our worry at this particular point is wasted energy.

I used to endeavor in this aimless pursuit of wondering and worrying about what others thought of me. Quite honestly, it still has some power over me, but not nearly so much as it used to, because I have discovered something most interesting.

When I was worrying what people were thinking about me, when I wondered whether it was good or whether it was bad, and when I actually inquired or asked what they were thinking about me, I learned they were not even thinking about me. Now that's important!

We needlessly exaggerate within our own reflection-cupboard the importance of what others think about us. We choose to give them too much power, especially considering the fact they probably are not even thinking about us.

Similarly, much of our concern over making mistakes is needless. Mistakes are not necessarily your villain.

We all make mistakes. It is my experience that on many occasions my mistakes have actually helped me with an audience. Instead of building barriers, mistakes can help speakers relate to and connect with audiences.

Speakers, like everyone else in the world, travel by detour. We make mistakes. Normally, our audience does not resent our stumbling, our minor miscues and our accidentally failing to secure noun and verb agreement. What an audience will resent, however, is a pseudo-perfectionism.

The members of the audience make mistakes. And they expect speakers to make mistakes. Of course, any strength taken too far becomes a weakness. We can make too many mistakes. *Celebrate The Butterflies* should certainly help you make fewer mistakes; but a few mistakes may not be all bad.

It is my experience, however, that many of us actually draw far too much attention to our mistakes. We cause our audience to focus on our mistakes far more than is necessary. It is as if we trip up and then telegraph our mistakes: "Oh, I'm sorry. Please forgive me. I did not mean to do that." Many times, these audiences say to themselves - "Do what?" They would not have even noticed that we did anything wrong, had we not telegraphed it.

So analyze your fear of looking at your audience. Then, it may not have the same degree of power over your eyes, over your face, over your body, over you. Remember to face it.

Your eyes and your face and your mistakes can actually help carry you into the listener's mind and heart.

Your Body Can Help

Your eyes and your face deliver you - your concern, your preparation, your sincerity, your warmth, your intensity, your passion and your purpose. Your body can help your eyes and your face!

Indeed, there should be a unity or consistency between what your eyes and face do and what your body does. Let your body express your intensity. It wants to do just that. Do not hold it back.

Forget Your Hands

"What do I do with my hands"? My students are always asking me that question, and I am repeatedly responding with "Forget them!" But, they will not listen.

One will speak ten minutes and the whole time keep his hands in his pockets. Your hands will not stay in your pockets unless you are thinking about them and deliberately choosing to keep them there. And, there deep in your pockets, they will never be able to work for you. If you focus on your hands, so focus on them that they remain deep within your pockets, your hands will be hurting you. But, if your forget your hands, forget them so much that they are freed out of your pockets, they will help you.

Another student will speak for ten minutes and the whole time keep her hands on the podium. Your hands will not remain on the podium for ten minutes unless you are thinking about them and deliberately choose to keep them there. And there, on the podium, they will never be able to work for you.

Forget your hands, and they will help you emphasize your points and your enthusiasm and your warmth and your personality. Forget your hands, let them do their thing.

Their thing is to extend your personality. Their thing is to extend you - you in all of your naturalness. Let them flip and flop as they will. It will be a beautiful and graceful thing for your audience to behold.

Forget your hands, and they will work for you. They will help you. Dwell on your hands, think about them all the time, and they will work against you. Keep them in your pockets or on the podium, and they will hurt you.

Podiums Paralyze

Speaking of podiums, I do not like them! Podiums paralyze!! They dilute the power of the body's presence.

Perhaps each of us has attempted to wash a car with a garden hose. For a while, the water is gushing from the hose. We move to the other side of the car and carry the hose with us. Now, water barely oozes out of the hose. What is the problem?

The problem is that the hose is crimped. The hose is twisted or constricted or closed at one point so that water does not completely flow through the hose.

Speakers dilute their power, crimp their style, impede the flow of their personality and the power of their message when they use podiums.

Podiums paralyze speakers. They hold them back. Podiums camouflage or cut off part of the power of one's presence.

Your whole body can work for you. But, if you position yourself there - hiding your body behind a wooden box, you paralyze your power, your personality, your capacity to move.

But I Need Somewhere To Put My Notes!

Each time I hear "but I need somewhere to put my notes," I seek to remind the speaker that one does not have to have notes.

Now, if you need notes, and there's certainly

nothing wrong with using notes, you can place the notes on a few large index cards. Either carry them with you or place them on the podium and glance at them from time to time. But please do not lean on the podium. If possible, do not even stand behind the podium. Podiums separate speakers from their audiences.

Note This

Speaking of notes, there are four different ways that you might choose to deliver your speech. The use of notes is only one of the four ways. For our purposes, notes will be referred to as "lists."

M And M And L And L

You can memorize your speech; you can deliver your speech from a manuscript.

You can deliver your speech aided by lists; you can learn your speech.

The above is arranged from the least desirable way of presenting your speech (memorized) to the most desirable way of delivering your speech (learned).

Speaking through lists is the second most desirable way to deliver your speech. The lists can actually help you learn your speech and hence possess a unique advantage over simple notes.

Memorized Versus Learned

I had rather hear a speech that is read than endure one that is memorized!

A speech can be an extension of life. It can be filled with passion. It can be blessed with personality. It can be influenced by both.

But it will not be filled with either passion or personality if it does not possess spontaneity.

From my experience, speeches that are memorized, robotical and mechanical appear false. Speeches that are learned, however, can be passionate, natural and powerful.

The First M

The first M stands for "Memorized." Please avoid it. Do not make your audience go through a memorized presentation. I believe most audiences would rather hear you read your speech than observe you go through some meaningless exercise.

Do not aim for a memorized speech. Aim for a learned speech. There is a difference, and the difference is naturalness. The difference is the very life of the speech.

Do not memorize! Learn.

The Second M

The second M stands for "Manuscript." The manuscript is your totally written-out or typed-out speech. When you do a manuscript presentation, you read your speech.

Many would argue that a memorized presentation is much better than one when the speaker merely reads the speech.

I am sure it is a matter of preference, (and I certainly think audiences prefer neither memorized nor manuscript presentations), but I had rather hear you read your speech.

But, if you can help it, and you can, please do not read your speech either. I cannot see your eyes when you read your speech. And remember, the audience wants to see your eyes and your face and your heart.

The First L

The first L stands for "Lists." Lists are triggers, bullets, concepts that make a road map for the speaker and for the audience.

I prefer the term "lists" over the term "notes" because lists refer to sequential movement, to order and to process. And sequential movement, order and process are fundamentally helpful in learning a speech.

Quite simply worded, speaking from lists of your bones and meat will help you learn, or conceptualize, not memorize your speech.

Furthermore, speaking through lists will help your audience visualize sequential movement, order and process, and hence learn your speech's fundamental theme.

When you speak from lists, you have before you the basic nuts and bolts of your manuscript's main points. You refer to these lists for help along the road of the delivery of your speech.

And, there is something wonderfully neat about this process. The more familiar you become with your lists, the easier it will become to see one item and then recall the others. Familiarity makes it possible for recall once you are provided the trigger that is revealed when you see something familiar on your list.

For example, if I am recounting for my audience several of the states in the southeast and I cannot remember any, I look down to my list and see "Georgia." Georgia serves as the trigger. Because I have practiced grouping Georgia with other key states, Florida, South and North Carolina, Alabama and Tennessee naturally come to my mind. Believe me, you can train your mind to do this.

For The Sell Speech, you will of course have five lists — the introduction list, body - level one list, body - level two list, body - level three list, and conclusion list. And, of course, underneath each umbrella you will have related lists.

The Second L

The second L stands for the "Learned" speech. Pay the preparation price, and it will really pay off!

The more familiar one becomes with one's lists, the closer one comes to presenting a learned speech.

Learn To Learn

But how does one learn "to learn one's speech"? One relaxes, and one utilizes what one already has.

Relax and utilize. Take a deep breath. Something nice is about to happen to you.

You probably know much more than you think you know about presenting in public. It is my strongly held theory that most of us do not present well, not because we do not know how, but because we block out what we do know.

You will experience a wonderful discovery when you unravel the difference between not being able to do something because you do not know how, and not being able to do something because you are unable to unleash what you do know.

The unleashing of what is within you has everything in the world to do with relaxation. I experienced afresh this very occurrence last week.

One particular young lady had been having more than minor difficulty in my public speaking course. She stumbled and hesitated incessantly until I discovered a fondness in her heart for horses.

Within minutes after this discovery, I asked her to do an impromptu presentation on caring for horses. She was marvelous!

Her timidity evaporated. A calmness captivated her and her audience.

A love for horses had been discovered deep within her. Now her fondness for horses was merely springing forth out from her personality into the audience.

She was allowing her familiarity with horses, indeed her passion for horses, to serve as a call for relaxation. Indeed, relaxation was befriending her, and she was relating well to the audience.

After her tremendous presentation, I asked her where her nervousness had gone. She smiled and indicated that she was not nearly as nervous. She thought her nervousness had left her.

I knew it had not. It was just that now her nervousness was working for her, helping her to relax.

Yes, nervous energy that is celebrated as friend is actively helping one to relax. Nervous energy that works as friend breeds relaxation and familiarity and effectiveness.

"Uh-ohs" do not have the same power. "Ah-has" are heard much more often.

It is right there in front of you; it will help you learn how to learn your speech. Find a passion, a topic; become very familiar with it. This will free you beyond your expectation.

Topic selection has everything in the world to do with familiarity. Familiarity breeds relaxation; relaxation breeds learning.

It May Be Right In Front Of You

Oh certainly, you may have to do a tremendous amount of research so you can build familiarity. I understand that.

But what I am trying to suggest here is that you already may be familiar with something about which you could speak. That something might be staring you in the face.

I will never forget what I saw at a rest area just off I-85 recently. People were standing in three different lines behind sinks in the men's restroom. The line behind the first sink was moving; it consisted of seven people. The line behind the second sink had five people; it too was moving rapidly. The line behind the third sink was one in number; it involved an elderly gentleman; it was not moving at all.

He just stood there; after a few moments, he looked at me and inquired why his sink did not have faucet handles.

What he did not know was that the other sinks did not have faucet handles either. But the other people knew that all they had to do was put their hands underneath the pipe; the water would automatically come on.

It was staring that gentleman in the face. His sink-pipe was right in front of him. But he did not know to put his hands under it.

Similarly, your passion may be staring you in the face. Your next topic, involving a subject with which you are unusually familiar, may be waiting for you to grab it.

Remember, do not miss it simply because it is right in front of you.

As I close this particular point, let me make a very sincere suggestion. If possible, when you deliver your next speech or your first speech, choose a topic that is very familiar to you. I think it will make it a whole lot easier for you to learn that next speech, or at least learn parts of it.

CHAPTER 10

Your Delivery Can Help You Emphasize

Be Sure They Know You Were Glad To Bake It

One of the more common mistakes my students make occurs when these students seek to accomplish everything within a singular speech. They try to get thousands of points across, and hence get nothing across.

If you can make a very few points, or even if you can just convey the basic fabric or theme of your presentation, you will be a big success. Your delivery can help you make those few points.

If you want to be a big success, if you want to deliver a meaningful presentation, think little. Get a theme over. Present an opportunity, a reason for the opportunity and present a response. Keep it simple. Emphasize something basic. Do not try to do too much.

Emphasize

Yes, your delivery can help you emphasize.

Let me share seven specific examples of how your delivery can help you emphasize your basic theme or emphasize your very few points. If you can learn these seven ways to emphasize, then your delivery will be once again helping you channel your nervous energy into friend, rather than enemy. To emphasize, learn to: punctuate, elevate, hyphenate, abbreviate, inundate, participate and celebrate.

Punctuate

Punctuate your words, your phrases, your sentences. Use commas, periods, question marks and exclamation points.

Your inflection, the variation in the tone of your voice, can help you emphasize.

If you have ever had children, I am sure you have punctuated for emphasis sake. The problem is that most of us punctuate when we are mad. We should also punctuate when we are glad!

Elevate

Lift your volume. Increase the loudness. Elevate the strength of your sound. Variation in volume serves as a wonderful tool of emphasis.

Hyphenate

Put a break in your sentences, in your phrases, in your thoughts. Pause!

Sometimes, the best way to say something is to say nothing. This hyphen, this pause, can certainly help you emphasize a point. Let me add that it is most potent when it is occasionally used, not overused.

If I sense that I'm losing an audience, I pause. If I want to especially catch their ear, I pause. If I really want to emphasize a point, I hyphenate, I pause!

Abbreviate

They remember nuggets, not boulders!

Brevity is a blessing. Many of us inappropriately think that excessive length, volumes of material, a very long speech equals emphasis.

Brevity will help you make a direct hit into and with your audience. Abbreviated, brief, precise and concise presentations will also allow you to channel your nervous energy into the chiseling or sculpting process.

It is when you break down boulders into nuggets, when you abbreviate, that you really make impressions. It is when you chisel, when you sculpt, when you abbreviate that you emphasize.

It is when you chisel, when you sculpt, when you abbreviate that you allow your nervous energy to work for you!

Inundate

To inundate is to repeat. Repetition is a strong emphasis tool.

But, like any strength, repetition taken too far becomes a weakness.

Nevertheless, if I want my audience to receive

the basic thrust of my speech, I must inundate them with sufficient exposures to and reminders of the basic reason why we are together.

Participate

If I want to emphasize the essence of my words, then my whole body, my entire delivery, must participate in symphony with my words. Remember, my eyes, my hands, my feet, my arms, my heart, all of my being must help me emphasize.

There are times when our whole body will want to come out in agreement with our words. There are occasions when our whole persona will want to participate in symphony with our words. When this happens, this is delivery at its best, this is emphasis!

Celebrate

Excitement is contagious. If I celebrate my point with every bit of my person, my audience is invited and encouraged to at least consider my point.

And, the beautiful thing here is that when I celebrate my point with my excitement, my nervous energy is working for me, not against me.

Remember to pour your nervous energy into your body, and as your body participates with your words, you will be encouraged to celebrate "the butterflies," to celebrate the good guys, to celebrate nervous energy.

CHAPTER 11

Delivery Distractions

It May Not Be The Baker's Fault

This particular segment of *Celebrate The Butterflies* is being drafted aboard a Delta jet headed from Philadelphia back to Atlanta. There are one hundred and sixty-four of us on this plane. Right now, and for the past thirty minutes, one hundred and sixty-three of us have been preoccupied with the one hundred and sixty-fourth of us.

That young tot, number one hundred and sixty-four, has been screaming her lungs out for one thousand and eight hundred seconds. With mechanical precision and an exceptional high pitch, her tones have reverberated within the plane. The current turbulence on the outside of the plane has taken second seat to turbulence inside the plane.

I am very aware that this precious one's distractive behavior will surely soon come to a halt. But distractions for the speaker will never come to a complete cessation. For that fact, distractions for the listener will never completely halt.

Simply worded, there are two types of distractions that can plague or challenge both speaker and listener. Just as our plane is now experiencing turbulence outside and turbulence inside, so must speakers and listeners experience both inside and outside turbulence or distractions.

Outside Distractions

When you speak, and when they listen, there will be turbulence outside. Expect it.

Babies will cry. Air conditioners will make noises. Pens will be dropped. Cars will speed by and rain will pour down; but you can hold your audience.

Outside distractions are challenges that can be overcome. You must first be aware that they will always exist; you must be prepared to work harder when they occur.

When the air conditioner comes on, increase your volume. When a baby cries, smile toward the baby and the mama. When something weird happens, and it will happen, spontaneously refer to it in a way that it may actually help explain your point.

Just as the quarterback calls an audible and changes the play even as he is calling signals, you may have to "audible" and change some of your calls as life unfolds even as you speak. But every appropriate modification will actually strengthen, not weaken, your speech.

Do Not Make Them Work Any Harder Than They Have To

Remember, the basic burden for overcoming outside distractions is yours, not the listener's. If outside distracting noise is birthed, either by an air conditioner, a motor, or a child aggravated by a wet diaper, you as speaker must be the one to work harder. That is your responsibility as speaker.

Do not put the audience into a position where they have to work harder or seek to listen more diligently to you.

When it comes to overcoming outside distractions, the speaker is the quarterback. The speaker is responsible for mandating the audible. The speaker is the one who has to work harder.

Remember, the audience is already competing against their own distractions.

Inside Distractions

Like outside distractions, inner turbulence is no stranger to speaker or listener. Inner distractions may be as minor as a sore throat or indigestion. Or the turbulence within may be as major as a broken relationship or a broken heart.

Speakers can overcome most minor inside turbulence, whether it be within the speaker or within the listener. Speakers can overcome some major inner turbulence within the speaker. And periodically the speaker may even be able momentarily to overcome distractions deep within a listener.

But for the most part, you will not always be able to overcome every distraction inside the listener's body, mind and heart.

Do the best you can here. But do not expect to win the eyes and ears and hearts of every listener every time. Sometimes the inside stuff is just too much; it may not be the baker's fault!

Acceptance of this fact will free you to do your best most of the time for most of your audience. Remember, you are not superwoman or superman, you are speaker. And speaker cannot control everybody's inside stuff.

I just want you to know that it will help you to be aware that inside stuff can keep a speech from being digested on the listener's part, even if that speech is well-written and well-delivered. Recognize this fact. Celebrate this fact. It will help you have more reasonable expectations of yourself and of your audience.

By far, most of the time your preparation will certainly make the difference. But sometimes, you could have prepared twenty times as much as you did prepare; a particular member of the audience would never have listened to a word you said. His inside stuff would have been just too much. Remember, all you can do is the best you can!

Part Four

Fly Butterfly Fly

CHAPTER 12

Fly Through The World Of Awkward

Awkward - "I'm up here. They are out there." Awkward - "They know more than I do." Awkward - "It won't come together!"

Speaking in public can indeed be awkward. Once you embrace this awkwardness, you can become the victor!

Yes, once you say to yourself that awkwardness is reality, then awkwardness does not have the same power over you. You become dominant over awkwardness.

I Am Up Here, They Are Out There!

Do not perceive yourself as one who is on exhibit. View yourself as a person in process of growth.

Do not give them excessive power over you. Allow them to help you grow. So what if you goof up? Do you really think they will all rush home and do nothing but incessantly talk about your goof?

Is your goal to impress them or persuade them?

If your goal is the former, to impress them, you will never reach the stage of ultimate impression. If your goal is the latter, to persuade them, you may be able to take significant steps toward that persuasion if you anticipate some awkwardness.

Just think of it this way, I am not on exhibit. I am in the process of growth. I am continuously growing from the caterpillar stage into a butterfly.

They Know More Than I Know

I have a friend who used to be a pastor of one of Atlanta's largest churches. One Sunday morning, his bishop surprised him at church. The bishop was one of several hundred seated in the congregation.

After the sermon, my friend told the bishop that he felt extremely awkward preaching in front of his bishop.

The bishop then told my friend, “I did not come to hear you preach, I came to worship.”

I have never been convinced that audiences simply come to hear speakers speak. They may not perhaps be coming to worship, they usually do come with their own agenda - and usually their agenda is growth.

Just because you know more than I know does not mean that I am unable to share something with you. The audience’s exposure to you may benefit the audience if you do not discourage yourself before you start. Please remember that you can benefit the audience in many ways, even if many of the audience know more about a particular topic than you know.

If you do nothing more than encourage members of your audience to continue feeling and behaving in a certain way, then your encouragement may have been very positive and helpful.

It Won’t Come Together!

This whole book would be a farce if it did not indicate how familiar I am with the feeling that can be categorized in any or all of the following terms: "I've been working on this speech for days, and I have made absolutely no progress!" "This is going nowhere." "None of this seems to be coming together."

Over the holidays, one of the children was incessantly beating at a huge stump. After about one hundred slashes into the wood, he seemed undaunted and continued to slash. Now his number of whacks at this red oak slab exceeded several hundred in nature. Finally, the chunk of wood split into two pieces. This twelve year old immediately jumped with joy!

He was excited about that last blow; that was the one that did it.

I knew better! I was excited about all the blows that had taken place before. I was excited about what had gone on before. I was delighted that he refused to give up, consistently plugging at the red oak chunk.

It is all that has gone on before that leads to the eventual accomplishment. In other words, accomplishment is influenced by the world of awkward! The world of awkward is something you should expect. Perhaps one day you may even embrace it.

Remember, you do not find confidence; confidence finds you. You will most likely find that confidence will discover you in the midst of the world of awkward.

Anticipate awkwardness. Learn to accept the inevitable.

Do not allow the world of awkward to terrify you. Let the world of awkward teach you.

Do not allow the world of awkward to overwhelm you. Overcome the world of awkward's total control over you.

Learn to work within the world of awkward!

CHAPTER 13

Fly Through Adrenaline Withdrawal

I want to warn you about this one!

This is the picture. You have worked exceptionally hard. You have dug deep into the mines of potential topics and have chosen one that suits you, your audience and the occasion.

You have prepared well, both at the point of writing the speech and delivering the speech. Your nervous energy has worked for you, not against you. Anticipation, not anxiety, is now your companion!

You're introduced; you begin to speak. Everything that you had hoped for is happening. You are immersed into your presentation. Your audience is listening and responding.

Come conclusion time, both you and the audience seem to be saying with every ounce of inertia that is within you - "this was worthwhile!"

The speech is over. Your adrenaline is now at its peak. That peak is nurtured by the audience sharing with you one to one, hand to hand.

But, wait a minute. They are leaving. The audience, your audience, is diminishing by the seconds. Within a matter of minutes, all that remains is the clean-up crew and you. Soon, you sit alone up front.

You are now totally alone. Even your adrenaline has left you!

This is normal. Expect this to happen. Remember, the drive to the celebration, and the celebration itself, are more exciting than the drive home.

Catch whatever you can and need out of this "aloneness." If, however, this "aloneness" is totally alien to you, allow it to service your next speech.

You have two choices at this point of adrenaline withdrawal. Either sit and rest, or stand and start planning your next speech. Either way, you should expect this to occur.

I recognize that this is a very brief chapter. I further recognize that it could have very easily been placed in the prior chapter, in The World of Awkward. But, I wanted this one to stand alone.

Adrenaline withdrawal happens! And face it, it should happen. Adrenaline withdrawal serves the body well!

CHAPTER 14

Fly Through Touchspeech

It is most important that you learn to touch an audience. It is equally essential that you as speaker allow the audience to touch you, to impact you.

This mutual-touching is not physical in nature. But, it is real. It is connectional, and it is relational.

Touchspeech transcends the level where one person is simply hurling a multitude of words toward an audience. Touchspeech moves beyond a mere mechanical release of sentences and paragraphs into a much more personal involvement between speaker and audience.

It is this very touchspeech that explains why members of audiences respond favorably.

> I have never felt like someone was talking directly to me like I did when I heard her speak.
>
> He touched me right at the core of my being. I forgot that I was one of several hundred. I felt like I was the audience.
>
> He was no machine, he was a person up there. He was down to earth and natural.
>
> His uniqueness blessed me. It is refreshing to be touched by a person who is so natural.
>
> Five minutes into the presentation, I sensed something different. There was a passion between her and her topic.
>
> Listening to him was not boring. It was exciting. He was so real. His 'realness' touched me. His enthusiasm was contagious!

And this same touchspeech justifies why many men and women speak. They will explain that they feel fed by the very fiber of an audience. Professional speakers will state that it is the relationship that develops with an audience during the speech that actually activates their adrenaline.

On a personal note, I like to refer to this phenomenon of touchspeech as a nurturing sort of event. I am fed by the audience.

I am nurtured by a smile, a head nod, laughter that turns into tears, and tears that culminate with a smile!

I'll never forget one of several presentations that I have made in Sioux Falls, South Dakota. There were approximately three hundred people in this audience. At the end of my speech, several members of the audience just sat there. And I wanted just to sit there. The audience seemed to be lost into the presentation.

I mean this in a very positive manner. The audience members, as well as myself, appeared to have been immersed into what had happened. "What had happened" was touchspeech!

I want to quickly add that this certainly does not always happen with me. But, on that day in Sioux Falls, it did.

I have appreciated every single standing ovation that has befriended me. But nothing has touched me like that particular experience.

I especially remember the look on one lady's face. Her look was not only a tribute to me, it was more emphatically a salute to the power of touchspeech! She seemed to be affirming the reception of something meaningful. She was also revealing her utter exhaustion!

Wow and Whew

It was as if my new South Dakotan friend was exclaiming both "wow" and "whew" at the same time!

Touchspeech is a paradox. It is both filling and emptying. It is both exhausting and refreshing. And, it impacts both speaker and audience.

Let me add, particularly if you are wanting to allow touchspeech to help you channel nervous energy into friend, that you will most likely experience touchspeech, either as speaker or audience, in the midst of a presentation that is persuasive in nature.

Touchspeech Happens

It occurs when the speaker is prepared, when the speaker has a passion for the presentation and when the speaker is himself or herself.

Preparation breeds an environment that invites touchspeech. Laziness, or sloppy preparation, repels any likelihood that touchspeech might occur.

Passion for a particular idea or persuasion can be contagious. A distanced, nonchalant, merely "going through the motions" attitude is something no one else would desire to catch.

The integrity of personality, a total consistency within oneself, will open the ears of the audience. Phoniness will quickly close those same ears.

Be prepared!

Be passionate!!

Be yourself!!!!!!!!!

CHAPTER 15

Fly Hand In Hand With Your Nervous Energy

It is time to mention Bo!

For more than a decade, this blonde, male Cocker Spaniel has blessed our home. Bo is mighty special.

Bo began his life twelve years ago with five senses. All but his sense of smell have long disappeared. Bo cannot hear you; he will never see you.

But Bo's sense of smell allows him to remain a faithful companion. To this day, Bo staggers his way behind me into the woods. Bo will always be there with me - unless he has dropped his tennis ball.

That tennis ball has become Bo's security blanket. Old age has intensified, not diminished, Bo's fascination with that ball of chartreuse.

If Bo loses his tennis ball, he feverishly hunts it down and snatches the ball back into his mouth. Bo does not want to let go of his tennis ball.

Just last week, I noticed that Bo was caught in a dilemma. It was suppertime. Just moments before, Bo had sniffed his way back to the lost tennis ball, retrieved the ball and returned to his spot in the garage. At that very moment, we served him his supper.

I will never forget what I saw. Bo was hungry; he tried to eat; but he would not let go of the tennis ball.

It was painful for us to watch Bo's struggle between keeping the ball in his mouth and adding food into his mouth at the same time. I firmly believe that Bo would still be hungry, had we not removed the ball. In spite of his hunger, Bo did not want to release the ball.

Bo did not want to let go!

Let Go!

Your train ride with your own nervous energy, and these techniques for baking and delivering a powerful speech-cake, should have encouraged you to let go of the idea that your nervous energy is against you.

Let go of the concept that nervous energy is villain. Digest fully the idea that, through preparation, your nervous energy can become your friend.

Let go of the idea that you have to achieve everything in one speech. Narrowcast. Be focused. Let go of the idea that volume always equals greatness. Remember, they recall nuggets not boulders.

Let go of the idea that podiums and excessive notes are essential. Podiums and volumes of notes can paralyze.

Let go of the idea that memorization is the way to proceed. Learn your speech.

Let go of the idea that it is enough to write a great speech. Remember, if you do not also deliver it effectively, they will never taste its deliciousness.

Let go of the idea that your adrenaline will always be activated at its highest level. Expect adrenaline withdrawal.

Let go of the idea that you will always reach everyone in the audience. Do your best.

Let go of the idea that excessive illustrations are the best way to operate. Excessive illustrations can camouflage your main focus.

Let go of the idea that the world of awkward is all bad. Expect awkwardness; then it will not have the same power over you.

Let go of the idea that thoughts will automatically stick with you. Write them down right then. Be leery of thought evaporation!

Let go of the idea that great speeches just happen. Let go of the concept that you can merely sit around and wait for happy endings and happy audiences. Prepare. I say again prepare!

The very fact that you have purchased this book indicates that you have a hunger. You desire to be a more effective speaker.

To satisfy your hunger, let go of the nervous energy that is your enemy. Take the hand of the nervous energy that is your ally.

Hand in hand, you and your nervous energy can fly — together!

Final Destination

Our time together began with a train ride. During the journey, you were given several opportunities to examine your nervous energy.

Hopefully you are ready to claim your nervous energy about speaking in public as friend. You can now be prepared to depart from relating to your nervous energy like a toddler or a teenager.

You no longer need to engage "the butterflies" in a way that is designed to catch and eliminate your nervous energy. Put away your tendency to be the toddler in relationship to your nervous energy.

It is no longer necessary for you to relate to "the butterflies" in a way that is designed to ignore your nervous energy. Put away your capacity to be the teenager in relationship to your nervous energy.

Now you can begin relating to your nervous energy as a grown child. You can depart the train, not as a toddler or teenager, but as a mature child.

You can "ooh and aah" every time your nervous energy helps you prepare. You can internally applaud every time nervous energy helps you participate in touchspeech.

You can acclaim nervous energy as an aid in blessing your speech with structure. You can laud your nervous energy for helping you create and deliver effective "just-as" stuff.

You can acknowledge your desire to embrace nervous energy gratefully for the way it helps you assemble, categorize, emphasize and even learn material. You can become a R-A-I-N-B-O-W person.

You can commend nervous energy for the way it works within you and for the way it is released from you - into the audience.

You can compliment nervous energy for the manner in which it befriends you with power; you can praise nervous energy for serving as a catalyst that actually helps project, not camouflage, your personality. As your best self, you can fly butterfly fly!

Now, upon reaching the final destination, you can endorse your nervous energy as a mighty force that merits celebration. You can celebrate "the butterflies!"

Notes

Chapter Two

- The quotation from Alexander Pope in Epistle to Dr. Arbuthnof used in Chapter Two was found in Bergen Evans, Dictionary of Quotations, New York; Delocorte Press, 1968, page 83.

Special Appreciation

In this section of notes, I would like to express my appreciation to two of my professors and to the authors of the textbook I have used for more than a decade.

Chapter Three

- Dr. Gerre Price of Mercer University's Department of Speech cared enough to confront me at the point of my laziness and served as a firm wall against my attempts at manipulating my way out of serious study of speech. Dr. Price was one of the first to teach me that caring could be exhibited in confrontation, as well as in affirmation. Dr. Price cared enough to refuse to applaud every time.

  Dr. Price was my wake-up call for preparation. I am indebted to her for insisting that I pay the preparation price. Her persistence has influenced my thinking on the value of preparation as discussed in Chapter Three.

Chapter Six

- Dr. Gordon Thompson of Emory University was a strong encourager. Dr. Thompson first introduced me to a speech organization paradigm similar to the one I described in Chapter Six.

Chapter Seven

- Speech: A Basic Text has served as the textbook for my speech classes over the years. Most recently, I have been using the third edition of this book: Robert C. Jeffrey and Owen Peterson, Speech: A Basic Text. New York: Harper and Row, 1989.

  I have placed it on my Recommended Reading list without reservation. I have especially appreciated the authors' discussion of informative supporting material. Their ideas have influenced my concept of "meat on bones" as discussed in Chapter Seven and my thinking about delivery as discussed in Chapter Nine.

Chapter Twelve

- Helpful reading in the area dealing with awkwardness can be found in M. Scott Peck, The Road Less Travelled. New York: Simon and Schuster, 1978, and in Stephen Gower, The Art Of Killing Kudzu - Management By Encouragement, chapter ten. Toccoa: Lectern Publishing, 1991.

The National Speakers Association

- Additionally, I would like to convey my appreciation for the National Speakers Association. There is no doubt that my membership in this organization has helped me develop as a speaker.

  The National Speakers Association mailing address is: 1500 South Priest Drive, Tempe, Arizona 85281. Their telephone number is: (602) 968-2552.

Visual Aids

- I have not discussed handouts, flip charts and other visual aids because I personally do not find them very helpful or necessary. I actually encourage my students not to use them because I believe that for many the use of visual aids is another attempt to evade or postpone the redirection of nervous energy.

However, many of you may be in a set of circumstances that will mandate the use of visual aids. Therefore, I have included in the Recommended Reading list books that will be of particular help in the utilization of visual aids.

Recommended Reading

Decker, Bert. You've Got To Be Believed To Be Heard. New York: St. Martin's Press, 1992.

Gower, Stephen M. The Art of Killing Kudzu - Management By Encouragement. Toccoa: Lectern Publishing, 1991.

Jeffrey, Robert C., and Peterson, Owen. Speech: A Basic Text. New York: Harper And Row, 1989.

Peoples, David. Presentations Plus. New York: John Wiley And Sons, 1988.

Peck, M. Scott. The Road Less Travelled. New York: Simon And Schuster, 1972.

Walton, David. Are You Communicating? New York: McGraw-Hill Publishing Company, 1989.

Additional Recommended Reading

With A Special Orientation Toward Future Trends

The public speaker benefits himself and his audience when he uses timely illustrations and material.

The one who speaks in public will be positively influenced by an awareness of future trends. Accordingly, this brief Recommended Reading list targeted toward those trends should prove to be helpful.

Cetron, Marvin and Davies, Owen. American Renaissance: Our Life At The Turn Of The Twenty-First Century. New York: St. Martin's Press, 1989.

Corbin, Carolyn. Strategies 2000. Austin: Eakin Press, 1986.

Drucker, Peter F. The New Realities. New York: Harper And Row, 1989.

Gerber, Jerry and Wolf, Janet and Klores, Walter. Lifetrends. New York: Macmillan, 1989.

Naisbitt, John and Aberdeen, Patricia. Megatrends 2000. New York: William Morrow And Company, 1990.

About The Author

Stephen M. Gower is nationally and internationally recognized as a specialist in management by encouragement and in the development of communication skills for leadership! His power-packed presentations have impacted hundreds of thousands of people. As founding president of The Gower Group, Inc., Stephen Gower has sculpted a human resource development company that is widely respected for high-energy keynote speeches and professional and unusually effective seminars.

Mr. Gower holds a bachelor's degree from Mercer University and a master's degree from Emory University. He has served, or is serving, on numerous state and regional boards, and is a member of the National Speakers Association. Mr. Gower's first book, The Art of Killing Kudzu - Management By Encouragement, has helped establish him as a national leader in management by encouragement.

Mr. Gower has taught public speaking on the college level for more than a decade. As a professional speaker, Mr. Gower is uniquely appreciated for his explosive enthusiasm and his compelling content! This rare blend of intensity and substance has led hundreds of organizations to invite him to speak.

Throughout the country, many associations, corporations, and communities have invited him back again and again.

As author, lecturer, consultant and conference speaker, Mr. Gower has developed eight different concepts that impact leadership and communication.

Mr. Gower is considered one of the country's most powerful speakers. His keynote speeches and seminars have impacted thousands of people across America and overseas.

The Gower Group, Inc.
P. O. Box 714
Toccoa, Georgia 30577
1-800-242-7404